KINGFISHER
An imprint of Kingfisher Publications Plc
New Penderel House
283-288 High Holborn
London WC1V 7HZ
www.kingfisherpub.com

First published by Kingfisher 2005
2 4 6 8 10 9 7 5 3 1

A CIP catalogue record for this book is
available from the British Library.

ISBN-13: 978 0 7534 1163 6

Printed in India
TS/0707/THOM/PICA(PICA)/90SHES/F

WHAT A HOOT!

over 150 HiLarious ANiMaL JoKES

Illustrated by **Martin Chatterton**

KINGFISHER

**Two goldfish were in their tank.
One turned to the other and said,**
"You man the guns, I'll drive."

**What books
do owls read?**
Hoot-dunits.

**What do you call an
illegally parked frog?**
Toad.

Two cockroaches were nibbling rubbish in an alley.

"I was in that new restaurant across the street," said one. *"It's so clean! The kitchen is spotless, and the floors are gleaming white. There is no dirt anywhere — it's so hygienic that the whole place shines."*

"Please," said the other cockroach, **frowning, "not while I'm eating!"**

A boy walks into a pet shop
and tells the pet shop owner
he'd like to buy a wasp.
"I'm sorry, sir, we don't sell wasps."
"Yes, you do! You've got
one in your window!"

**Why do gorillas
have big noses?**
*Because they have
big fingers!*

What's a polygon?
A dead parrot.

What has four legs and an arm?
A happy pit bull.

What do you get if you cross a hedgehog with a stinging nettle?
Extremely sore hands.

First cow: Moo.

Second cow: Baa.

First cow: What do you mean, "baa"?

Second cow: Oh, I'm learning a foreign language.

Why is it difficult to hold a conversation with a goat?
It always butts in.

A man brought his dog to the vet. "I'm really worried about him," he said. "I dropped some coins on the floor and before I could pick them up, he ate them." The vet advised him to leave his dog there overnight. The next morning, the man called to see how his dog was doing. The vet replied, "No change yet."

"I've just bought a pig."

"Where are you going to keep it?"

"Under my bed."

"But what about the smell?"

"Oh, I'm sure the pig won't mind it."

A duck went into a chemist's and asked for some ointment.

"Certainly," said the chemist, "Shall I put it on your bill?"

What did the horse say when he reached the end of his nosebag?

That's the last straw.

What does a bat sing in the rain?

"Raindrops keep falling on my feet."

Why do bees hum?

Because they don't know the words.

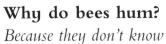

A man went to visit a friend and was amazed to find him playing chess with his dog. *"I can hardly believe my eyes!" he exclaimed. "That's the cleverest dog I've ever seen."* **"Oh, he's not so clever," the friend replied. "I've beaten him three games out of five."**

What did the beaver say to the tree? *"It's been nice gnawing you."*

What do you get when you cross a cat with a vacuum cleaner?
I don't know, but it drinks a lot of milk.

What's worse than taking a bite of your apple and seeing a worm there?
Seeing half a worm.

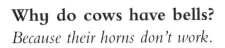

Why do cows have bells?
Because their horns don't work.

What goes trot-dash-trot-dash-dash?
Horse code.

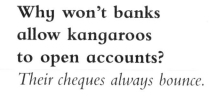

**Why won't banks
allow kangaroos
to open accounts?**
Their cheques always bounce.

**Why did the
chicken cross
the clothes shop?**
*To get to the
other size.*

First Rhino: What's that creature over there?

Second Rhino: That's a hippopotamus.

First Rhino: Fancy having to live with an ugly face like that!

What do dogs call parking meters?

Pay toilets!

What did the mother buffalo say to her son before he left?
Bison.

Why did the dog cross the road twice?
He was trying to fetch a boomerang.

Why do polar bears have fur coats?
They don't look good in tweed ones.

What did the flea say to his friend just before they went to the cinema?

"Shall we walk or take a dog?"

How do you know there's an elephant under your bed?

Your nose is touching the ceiling.

**What do you get from
a well-educated oyster?**
Pearls of wisdom.

**Where do dogs
go when they lose
their tails?**
To the retail store.

**How can you tell if an elephant is
getting ready to charge?**
He pulls out his credit card.

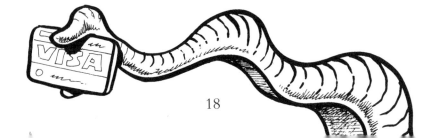

How can you tell a cat from a comma?
A cat has claws at the end of its paws, and a comma's a pause at the end of a clause.

What do you call a fly with no wings?
A walk.

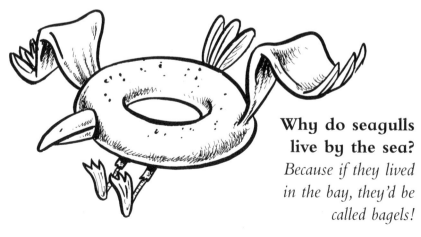

Why do seagulls live by the sea?
Because if they lived in the bay, they'd be called bagels!

Why did the dog owner think his pet was a master mathematician?
Because when he asked what zero divided by six came to, the dog said nothing.

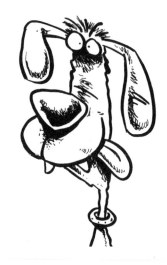

What do you get if you cross a turkey with a banjo?
A bird that plucks itself.

What's grey, has big ears and a trunk?
A mouse going on holiday.

What do you call a frog with no hind legs?
Unhoppy!

What do you get if you cross a dog with a telephone?
A golden receiver.

What do you give a seasick elephant?
Lots of room.

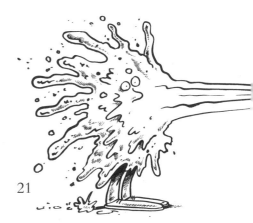

21

A large sailing ship was at anchor off the coast of Mauritius, and two dodos watched as a group of sailors rowed ashore.

"We'd better hide," said the first dodo.

"Why's that?" asked the second.

"Because we're supposed to be extinct, silly."

Waiter, there's a fly in my soup!
Well, throw it a pea and it can play water polo.

What do you call a cow with no feet?
Ground beef.

**Why are dogs such
bad dancers?**
They have two left feet.

**How do hedgehogs
play leapfrog?**
Very carefully.

**What's worse than a giraffe
with a sore throat?**
A centipede with verrucas.

**What's the definition
of an insecticide?**
A suicidal fly.

**"Have you ever seen
a man-eating tiger?"**
*"No, but I did once see
a man eating chicken."*

"Mummy," said the baby polar bear,
**"Are you sure I'm 100 percent pure
   polar bear?"**
*"Yes, of course I'm sure! What a silly question.
  I'm a polar bear and so is your father.
  Why do you ask?" said the mother bear.*
"Because I'm flipping freezing!"

**How can you tell
which spiders
are the trendiest?**
*They have their
own websites.*

**What do you put
on a pig's pimple?**
Oinkment.

What goes "quick, quick"?
A duck with hiccups.

"I have to write an essay on elephants."
"You'll need a ladder."

Which bird is always out of breath?
A puffin.

What do you get if you cross an elephant with a sparrow?

Broken telephone wires.

How do you get five donkeys in a fire engine?

Two in the front, two in the back and one on the roof going ee-aww ee-aww.

**What do you call a
pig that does karate?**
Pork Chop!

**Why did the dinosaur
cross the road?**
*Because the chicken hadn't
been invented then.*

**Which farm animal
talks too much?**
Blah Blah Black Sheep.

**What do you call
a fish with no eyes?**
A fsh.

**Why did the hedgehog
squeal "Ouch, ouch,
ouch!"?**
*Because he put his coat
on inside out.*

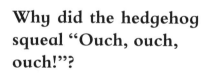

**What never shows off
about making honey?**
A humble bee.

What happened when the dog went to the flea circus?
He stole the show.

What's the hardest thing about learning to ride a horse?
The ground.

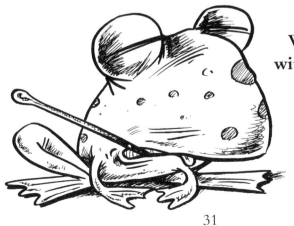

What's green with red spots?
A frog with chickenpox.

Why did the koala bear fall out of the tree?
Because he was asleep.

Why did the second koala fall out of a tree?
Because he was holding the first one's hand.

Why did the third koala fall out of the tree?

Because he thought it was a game.

What's grey and goes round and round?
An elephant in a washing machine.

What do you get if you cross a dog with a skunk?
Rid of the dog.

What happened to the glow-worm when he was squashed?
He was de-lighted.

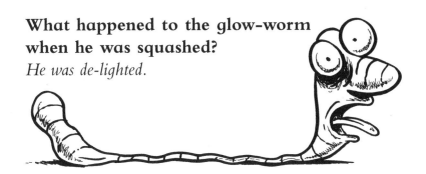

How do you get rid of termites?
Exterminite them.

What do you call a sleeping bull?
A bulldozer.

How do you stop a dog from being sick in the back of the car?

Put it on the front seat.

What do you get if you cross a rabbit with shallots?

Bunions.

How many insects are needed to fill an apartment block?
At least ten ants.

What game do cows play at parties?
Moosical chairs.

What happened to the two bedbugs who fell in love?
They were married in the spring.

**What has four wheels,
gives milk and
eats grass?**
A cow on a skateboard.

**What did the frog say
at a dinner party?**
*"Time's fun when you're
having flies."*

Why do dogs run in circles?
It's hard to run in pentagons.

Why are giraffes so slow to apologise?
It takes them a long time to swallow their pride.

Who lost a herd of elephants?
Big Bo Peep.

39

Why don't hippos ride bicycles?
The helmets don't fit them.

Customer: Do you have alligator shoes?
Clerk: Yes, sir. What size does your alligator take?

Two snails robbed a tortoise. The policeman asked, "Can you describe the thieves?"
"No," said the tortoise, "it all happened so quickly."

A dog walked into the post office and asked the clerk to send a telegram. He wrote down the telegram he wished to send: "Bow wow wow, Bow wow wow."

The clerk said, "You can add another 'Bow wow' for the same price."

"Yes, I know," the dog replied, "but wouldn't that sound a bit silly?"

Why don't penguins fly?
They're too small to reach the controls.

What do you get when you cross a centipede with a turkey?
Drumsticks for everybody!

Why did the fly fly?
When the spider spied her.

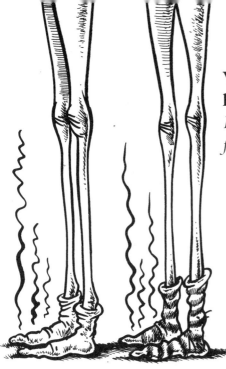

Why do giraffes have long necks?
Because their feet smell.

What do you have to avoid if it rains cats and dogs?
Stepping in a poodle.

A man took his Rottweiler to the vet and said to him, "My dog's cross-eyed. Is there anything you can do for it?"

"Well," said the vet, "let's have a look at him."

The vet picked the dog up and had a good look at its eyes. Eventually, he shook his head.

"I'm sorry, I'm going to have to put him down."

"Just because he's cross-eyed?" said the man.

"No, he's heavy," said the vet.

What do you call a chicken who crosses the road, rolls around in mud and then comes back?
A dirty double-crosser.

What type of shoes do frogs wear?
Open toad.

What do you do when a pig has a heart attack?
Call a hambulance!

What do you call bears with no ears?
B.

How do you know if there's an elephant in your fridge?
Footprints in the butter.

What kind of fish do you find in a birdcage?
A perch.

**What do you get
if you cross a
dog and a frog?**
A croaker spaniel.

Boy snake: Dad, are we poisonous?
*Daddy snake: Of course we are, son, why
do you have to ask?*
Boy snake: I've just bitten my tongue.

What's grey and white on the inside and red on the outside?
An inside-out elephant.

How do you identify a bald eagle?
All his feathers are combed over to one side.

What do you call a chicken in a shell suit?
An egg.

Two goats were out behind a cinema, eating old movie film. One goat said to the other, "Pretty good, huh?"
The second goat said, "Yeah . . . but it's not as good as the book."

What kind of bird
can write?
A pen-guin.

What did the donkey who only had weeds to eat say?
Thistle have to do.

What do you give a sick canary?
Tweetment.

What happens when two snails have a fight?
They slug it out.

THEY DON'T CALL ME THE DEMON HUNTER FOR NOTHING.

Now, *that* is my kind of story...

You know that thing they say about pins dropping? How you can hear them? It was a bit like that when Becky stopped speaking.

We all stared at her. She stared back, and then she said, *'What?'* and we all just went on listening for that pin.

Oh, my!

Why can't two elephants go swimming at the same time?

They only have one pair of trunks.

What do you call a polar bear wearing earmuffs?

Anything you like – he can't hear you.

What do you get when you cross a penguin and an alligator?
I don't know, but don't try to fix its bow tie!

Why is it dangerous to do sums in the jungle?
Because if you add four and four, you get ate . . .

Where do cows go on holiday?
Moo York.

Young boy: Can I buy some birdseed please?
Owner: How many birds have you got?
Young boy: None – I want to grow some.

What do you get if you cross an elephant and a kangaroo?
Big holes all over Australia.

Why do birds fly south in winter?
It's too far to walk.

What do snakes like to study at school?
Hisssstory.

What did the frog order at the fast-food restaurant?
French flies and a diet croak.

Where do ponies go when they're ill?
The horse-pital.

Why are fish so clever?
They live in schools.

Why did the flea lose its job?
It wasn't up to scratch.

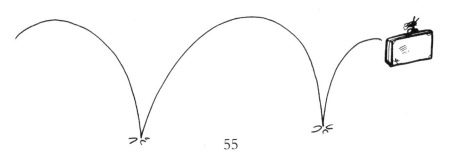

**What's grey, has big
ears and goes
squeak-squeak?**
*An elephant wearing
new shoes.*

**What's black and white
and eats like a horse?**
A zebra.

**What do you get
if you cross a
toad with
a galaxy?**
Star warts.

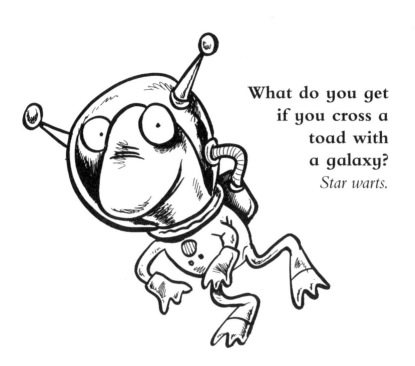

**What happened to the
shark who swallowed
a bunch of keys?**
He got lockjaw.

**What do you call a sheep
with no legs or head?**
A cloud.

**When is the best time
to buy budgies?**
When they're going cheep.

**What do you call
a cat eating a
lemon?**
Sour puss.

**Why did the lion
lose at poker?**
*Because he was
playing with
a cheetah.*

**What kind of bears
like bad weather?**
Drizzly bears.

**What happened to the dog
who ate nothing but garlic?**
His bark was worse than his bite.

**Man: Can I have a parrot
for my son, please?**
*Pet shop owner: Sorry, sir, we
don't do swaps here.*

How much did the psychiatrist charge to see an elephant?
£550. It was £50 for the visit and £500 for a new couch.

What do you give a sick snake?
Asp-irin.

What has antlers and sucks blood?
A moose-quito.

**What did the slug
say as he fell off
a branch?**
How slime flies.

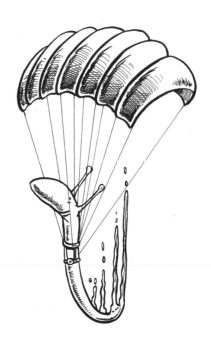

**What's the difference between
a flea and a wolf?**
*One howls on the prairie; the other
prowls on the hairy.*

Why did the owl say "Tweet, tweet"?

Because she didn't give a hoot.

Other titles in the *Sidesplitters*
series for you to enjoy: